Esa's Fables

Esa's Fables

RICARDO "ESA" GIULIANI

ESA'S FABLES

iUniverse books may be ordered through booksellers or by contacting:

iUniverse
1663 Liberty Drive
Bloomington, IN 47403
www.iuniverse.com
1-800-Authors (1-800-288-4677)

ISBN: 978-1-5320-5183-8 (sc)
ISBN: 978-1-5320-5184-5 (e)

Print information available on the last page.

iUniverse rev. date: 06/07/2018

The Life and Times of a Visionary Poet in Hiding

€SA'S FABLES A collection of original poems designed to take readers on a unique journey into time, transcend all manner of conscious thought, and view images of the collective unconscious in evolutionary species, that resists alien/human reality.

Poetry is another direct path taken in search of truth, an illusive manmade truth, which over centuries of deliberate religious deception, has created untold mental roadblocks in humanity: reducing human thought to a state of spiritual blindness.

Visionaries have always appeared at critical times through human history to revive emotional devolution in spiritually declining cultures. These unusual personalities have tried to offer hope to a failing dominant civilization of the times, and as the history of mankind has proven, carriers of an eternal truth are rejected in that quest

Even in my college years, which passed much too quickly, I was considered a spiritual comfort to others as a musician, playwright, poet, and artist. My creative energies went far beyond the parameters set by academic guidelines.

Such as it was then, as it is now, my singular most important task is in universal spiritualism.

Life gives natural cause for me to be both student and teacher, willingly, this is what find serenity in comfort given, from centuries of alien/human existence.

Every facet of my personality is an open expression of my beliefs, which gives further reason for publication of these works. Hopefully, in these works, others might find cause to begin the search for alien spiritual energies, that reside within our collective unconscious existence. Christ-consciousness is an eternal reality.

Esa

A Different Drum

tap, tap, tap, dry lips begin to flap
about the rain
praying happier times
are
on the way

what can you say
tomorrow is another day
a stale cliché'
to those living on borrowed earth time

happiness
is
compact and deranged
glorious
in
verbal exchange over precepts of insanity

the sun rises early in the twilight zone
shining seas 'n' raging foam
dedicated to
classic stories of the rich

a celestial matrix
in
time and space
reminds us anew of the race
against
well-known clocks of biblical prophecy

why do mortals
march to a different drum in such abstract random order?

Peace & love sent from wherever heaven is above
Described
By
Eyes focused on the past.

True believers totally aghast at the terrible sight
an astronomical cost
when all is lost
forever gone & never to return.

Spiritual futility at best as the rest of the world
stands mockingly shunned
caught behind
a stunned & silent wall of disbelief.

… Charlatans & thieves side-by-side making unbreakable rules …

Spiritual ghouls & fools with faulty explanations
hiding all holy truth from view
renewed in the hope
no one sees the forest for the trees.

Remnants of a legend hidden in secret archives
hated & despised by true disciple
of
The Great Liar
insisting truth doesn't exist.

Progenitors in a final reprise luxuriate & surmise
the truth will surpass
anything
previously known to mortal man.

It has been said by lesser gods
love will conquer all
I believe

the 20th century "mark of the beast" was perceived as a sign of the times.

A Well Known Bedtime Story

Once upon a time in a mythical land far away
terrible night creatures roamed
through
the world of dreams.

Long, long ago, the coldness of an arctic blast
cast our celestial angels
upon
a desperate scene.

It was you they had finally come to see
you on fragile knees
in
dire need of spiritual repairs.

God know the needs
of
those praying for deeds larger than themselves.

~Prayers of a supernatural nature could not be answered ~

Faith is in eternal truth
that gives hope
nothing like those goofy soap operas
life isn't some sill spoof or joke, only faith in action.

Year by year time moves ahead
no one tries
out of fear and dread
simple ways to understand amazing mysteries.

Look into the future of dreams, illusions and phantasies
while standing on
the threshold to the 21st century.

In the twinkling of an eye
you shall see
the last one to leave the 20th century ~and ~ who turns out the lights.

America:
A Monumental 911 Theme Park

The Koran says: "Kill or be killed," The Bible says: "Thou shall not kill."
North- South -East- West
find which way is the best, as you travel along spiritual roads
carefully marked neutral zones, white hot desert
sands, bushes, that begin to blaze.
Give another unborn child a chance for life, no pro-choice
denied watch as the little ones make angels in the snow
watch them grow, how fast time goes.
War declares no holidays, quickly good times fade, then die away.
Teenage years, music dreams, Peggy Sue, me and you, family ties abide
happiness resides, happily laughing, then children cried! Why?
••• Because preachers lied to them, about Jesus! •••
Wow, let us seize one last chance, to change
those foul-mouthed TV channels.
STOP/GO: Ides of March - Income Tax - Memorial
Day - Labor Day - Thanksgiving Oh, gracious sakes alive,
another Julian calendar year is spent, pay the rent
don't forget about Candlemas; now a valued
money day as Christmas, what a waste.
Aside from all this falsified freedom maze, take
time to pause, give heavenly thanks.
In the words of a song: "Oh, it's a long, long way, from May to
December and days grow short, as you reach September."
September 11, 2001: A Space Odyssey
A day that lives in infamy, an insidious grand circle, an American Dream
machine an unholy encasement in uniformity, for "god remembrance day"
another chaotic way, to preserve theme park
attractions, on this planet Earth.
Huddled masses, it was your clarion call, might
makes right, fight to be free!

••• What does that mean? •••
I don't think I understand the context!
Did someone change our ancient/eternal blueprint for human survival?
If medieval armor was stripped away from the
man, you would find a "little boy."
No, not the nuclear bomb, a manmade standard of comparison
so carry on wayward sons, in strict obedience, to all inherited ground rules.
What is war good for? Absolutely nothing! Who said that? It wasn't me!
It was one brightly shining star, who did release, love and peace
in his own words, to understand the beast, thanks go out to Edwin Starr.
Learn from past mistakes, so much to live for,
no risk, the biological clock is ticking.

AMERICA: A MONUMENTAL 911 THEME PARK
••• An award winning 21st century three act comedy •••
The Fellowship of the Rine;~ The Two Towers ~ The Return of the Kin2

Awaken Dreams Of Tomorrow

In a world far away, or so it seems far away
from day-to-day reality
unreasonable
to reach
an unreachable goal
to know the inner beauty of kindness.

Once again, so far away, gazing into a warming smile
an unrealistic world
one created
by an adventuresome mind
in hidden meanings of suppressed warmth.

When again, if ever shall I know, such unselfish charm
when the winds move quietly
spraying gentle mist
on such
a common day
resisting temptation, to say uplifting words.

Seen as hushed tones beneath my breath, inside my mind
the words keep gushing forth
but none are spoken
like
broken glass
impossible to reassemble without pain.

Like every dream about tomorrow, images fade into time
even to one who dares to dream
nebulous, vague, unclear
what do I see
when I close my eyes
what disguise will I set upon myself this day?

If I refrain, would someone know, can I keep this secret hidden in the mist?

Celestial Vibrations, Another Time, Another Place

Desperation without reason or cause
plays into life
a spear into the side of mortal man
agonizing over self-made dilemmas of a vengeful nature.

Never again shall man be called to serve
a noble purpose
too much hormonal forgetful remembering
when the sword of destruction is greater than any cause.

We came in peace to clear the path of eternal truth
unsurpassed in glorious faith
side-by-side
set in uncompromising struggles with time.

Time, a meaningless form of human exaggeration
cast into the void
nothingness, endless nothingness
set beyond the boundaries of any formless arrangement.

Can inner visions scan an alienated soul to hear the cries of others?

Past lives are wrapped tightly to a world of endless torment
seeking mindless truths
telling endless lies
waiting on tormented troublesome dreams
while fighting for the right to be heard above the masses.

Where is this cause for wich one risks future love
so many temptations there
where they have existed throughout each siege
unforgiving along lines marking undefined time and space.

Happiness, another sad array of passing days searched for in vain
lost in the closeness of desperate fears
scattered about a world
where each new day accommodates adjudicated suffering.

Celestial vibrations, another time, another place
where then is pain so great, that truth cannot
comfort, nor spiritual love heal?

Deeds Of Daring Do

it's no sin, but once again, it's just me
squeezing
through the cosmic door.

i pray you're not offended
and
haven't blended into the woodwork of life.

may strife beseech you not
and
may you cast your lot among the very wise.

no one can judge your deeds
while you
go about planting seeds of greater things to come.

from where i stand, there is no hallowed land
only
sounds of a churning sea.

but of course, what seems to be worse
is
I am lost in time.

good things come alive
for those
with that unshakable will to survive.

... so virtue leads me to deeds of daring do, for which i'm famous ...

Designer Genes

See that guy over there, beware: The man has a Holy Book
he will make you pay.
Why?
Because you are afraid.

Don't betray yourself to him out of fear, don't let him get too near.

OK, so you think it's all right, he might know something
I don't know
that doesn't surprise me in the least.

Nothing I can say, will turn you away, from the words of his Holy Book.

Who said: When you're dead, it's fun to live?
Now, that's a strange look
it doesn't hurt
listening and learning all you can.

Take a good look at that man, change the words, you change the meaning.

There must be a hidden message somewhere here
now tell me
I am deranged
mathematical codes in the cradle?

Flower power man, what happened there, they're still running scared.

Mom and dad, still living in their self-made hell
all is well
one moral lesson here
neither one found their soulmate.

Oh yeah, a word of caution about the Holy Man, and his Holy Book:

Your heart is exposed, the brain transposed
I hear the sound of a crucifix, and it's still ticking.

Well, there is nothing more to say, designer genes, do weaken human knees.

DONUTS FOR AMERICA

Summertime, living is easy, fish are jumping, no cotton in the fields
the cotton is in Hanes underwear
made in Mexico
I guess the reality is
no one sees a reason for 20/20 vision.

Call it what you will, land of the free, home of the brave
Pleasure Island with its Pinocchio
Fantasy Island with its Mr. Roark
we should pop the cork after a UFO sighting
Butterscotch Elephant Farm, whatever, or wherever it is?

BMW factory, no welfare checks there, it's baby boomer heaven
meanwhile on planet Earth
a million strawberry alarm clocks
ring in empty rooms, another day in the life New Year.

Cookies w/white icing on the L.A. freeway, thin crust pizzas on Wall Street
American automobiles with Japanese names
oriental workers
riding bicycles on crowded streets, the 21st century is here.

Burger King wrappers
beneath
McDonalds' golden arches
Wendys' pigtails caught in the teller's window at the bank.

What's that out-of-date saying we used to live by:
United we stand and divided we fall?

It's worse
when we bicker
the lady on the water cries, as the torch begins to flicker.

In your wildest dream, did you really think, this was the good life, Bunky?

DZZZD MINDS

I know it isn't fair to compare, right from wrong
I sense deep despair
when someone shares family secrets.

It isn't right to ask too many questions, I am told
advice is free
it's strange for me to see
instant family replays, as naked truth.

I guess you've heard, lions hide in sheep's clothing
cover your eyes
this has no disguise
because every rose has its thorns.

Take a number, when you enter, a day care center.
Wanna know why?
No one
will remember who you are tomorrow.

What was the total body count today, did someone display
too much affection?

Why must love always be, so weird and strange?
Why do adults
arrange facts, to fit their own needs?

Will we awake in time, to save the child, we left behind?
Who has spread

these artificial seeds of lasting doubt?

I know rules are made by fools, it makes perfect sense
total control — does fan the fires of hate.

It is a long and winding road, with detour signs
leading to spiritual blindness
there seems to be a lack of kindness, in the heart and soul of Dzzzd Minds.

Empty Spaces

No one realizes, I am a child
much younger
than I was before, many, many years ago.

This is deemed so by the grace of God
though it seems odd
to
comprehend.

My life fits together in celestial time
designed
to
make me smile.

No laws can exist between love 'n' hate
I pray aloud
to
feel the power of faith.

… Guardian angels bathe in amazing waters …

I am blessed, yet I don't know why
I try to understand
demands
made on me.

It always feels so strange inside
as
even now
a mortal curse resides.

This time spent on earth
must be
a myriad of mathematical stumbling blocks
flesh 'n' bone abated by life, watching as empty spaces disappear.

.. Yesterday, today, tomorrow, there are all the same ...

One difference
when
passion for life
allows the natural mind
its place and design, in a world going mad, from its hatred.

Remember one thing, and remember it well
emotional prisons
are ruled
by superstition and fear.

These can be life sentences
carried out
inside
a dark and haunted cell formation.

Without ethics to live by, the artist, in the human mind
day-to-day
S
L
O
W
L
Y
paints a portrait of Dorian Gray
with the signature of the artist, to give it realism, from canvas to skin.

Evening News

Media Elves sent the evening news around the world
The shroud image of Christ disappeared
Gone without a trace
Santa Claus land was shaken coast-to-coast.

Christmas chains began to rattle
As ghosts haunted cash registers everywhere
Striking fear into the heart and soul of true believers.
The one day a year "Peace On Earth" master plan
Went on interplanetary red alert.

In the official North Pole news center
Santa Claus spread rumours of an alien abduction.

Rabbi Greenwitz placed protest signs in synagogues
JESUS
Accept no substitutes

Christians of all faiths across America
Demanded an immediate explanation of the situation.

Due to intense world-wide religious criticism
About the real origin of Christmas
Media Elves asked for cancellation of all future birthdays.

Henceforth, in an attempt to end massive global conflicts
The colorized version of "It's a Wonderful Life"
Will replace the 6:30 news.

This was found acceptable by most major networks
But only until a new millennium standard has been established.

Feeble Minds

Should you pray, or should you merely, pay the price
to live in the house of glass
that
your fictitious Jesus built for you.

So, what has happened to this whirligig religious zeal
no sex appeal
get Jesus a woman to love
he can't be an American Idol, that's covered.

Yeah man, I have heard, however absurd, the dead shall live again.

Hey, fill me in on stories about Jesus, like mom and dad
it's sad
kids don't care anymore
their either wrapped in sex, or rapping to get sex.

"Born again Christians," now there's a wild goose chase
it's the ace in the hole
just like
taking out a life insurance policy.

Insurance companies betting you die, you're betting you won't, Hmm.

As the world turns upside down, and inside out, spiritually lost
I ask a simple question:
What is the cost of religious salvation?

Shout aloud, brethren of the cross, ridiculed and tossed about
usually three sheets in the wind
too much
sacramental wine, for one sinner to drink.
Feeble minds have feeble ways, so the good book says
this mythical story ends
with a beast, feasting on the brain of modern man, obsessed by primal ways.

Flies in the Ointment

Hold the banner high my son
Against the glare of a fiery new dawn
Live the fun of frolicsome youth one on one.

Take your hands from deaf ears
Listen to the wise man before you run ...

A warm hello and a sad goodbye
Makes you smile and makes you cry as one
Melancholy and nostalgia spark frolicsome fun.

Remember, the blind man sought youth
After he grew too old to believe ...

Teach the world you love to understand.

Focus your eyes on a good earth
Filled with compassion and a healing mirth

In matters of the heart
God demands proof there are flies in the ointment

.

Footnotes to History

Might I indulge you for a brief moment in time
while we access my mind
and the few scattered thoughts still there.

Historians say it's unrealistic to pretend to know
all there is to know
about
conditions in our tethered world.

Precluded from the past for so long a time
reminds me
of
another story I would like to tell.

It's not the differences between heaven and hell
no words difficult to spell
no emotions
as
I write an epic story in abbreviated form.

Phantasies combine to make me a living soul again
another spin off on a new theme
interpretation of dreams
censored legions of my nightly trek into time.

Questions will arise as to what I am talking about
let the records show
I am not
the man who sold the world.

Looking for answers
has become
a virtual tailspin against the winds of time
infinite resources coated by primordial slime are on footnotes to history.

Heart-to-Heart

(The world through Mary's eyes)

Through pleading eyes and searching mind
hope-on-hope
and
yet to find the truth.

A thousand years has passed before my eyes
or
so it seems
I'll put my schemes behind me.

The days of longing, the days of pain
voices in your head
somehow
everything feels right again.

Forever takes so long and mortals cannot wait
destiny belongs to someone else
in my mind
I simply call it fate.

I've traveled far on unfamiliar roads
and
paused along the way
alone now on a trek in time, it's easier to pray.

… The light of love will guide my steps, 'til we are heart-to-heart …

House Of Glass

Sketch in today as the unknown factor
explore it
to the depth of its character.

A single brush stroke
of
the heart
a touch of love to adorn life.

A house of glass
within
the confines of human ways.

Windows Doors Walls Ceilings
all
perspectives in time.

The fragile blueprint is invisible
while
inside looking out.

... do not throw stones ...

A miracle house built on trust
may shatter
and
the beauty of its reality is lost forever.

Abstract surrealism in nature
clings to life
in
autumn tones of faded glory.

How self-righteous they seem, as storm clouds gather, over a house of glass.

I Guess I've Said Enough

... Hello again ...

I know I seem distant and vague
I do beg
your forgiveness.

I know what I'm trying to say
and
it eludes me so easily.

It's just that
I cannot put the puzzle together again.

I lost the instruction manual
and
pieces don't fit anything I recognize.

I suppose
I must be doing something wrong.

Do I get more than one try?

The first few times was easy
before
the rules changed.

I think I will quit, while I am still ahead.

Well, it's getting daylight, I guess I've said enough.

Isn't Life Strange

keys turn in every lock
as
shockwaves
puncture human brain cells

how near, yet so far
we seem to be
from the transcendental reality we seek

herald angels sing, as flapping wings
slap against our head
so it must be said, we are more dead, than alive

... portals in time, allow us this fragmented realism ...

mental landscapes of frozen waters
from past lives
overflow banks of our shallow emotional creeks

metaphysical and remote
So little hope
floating in endless space, sprinkling stardust

behold
the man
who spanned the centuries
in
peace
&
love
he only increased the flames of fragmented realism

keys turn n every lock, in mock concern I ask ... isn't life strange?

Karma

Place the burden of proof upon yourself
one negative act at a time
an unnatural kind
causing others human pain and strife
cutting like a knife, into the heart of love and understanding.

Lovingly deceitful or spiteful, if you will it openly, it is karma in action.

Without thinking, scream and shout, crazed empty words
senseless reason (or) senseless doubt
shattering the lives of others
while scattering all hope of spiritual redemption to the wind.

When you rearrange mortal sin, holding arms seductively outstretched
whether pretentious (or) conscience free, as wretched be
mindful, but forgetful, with eyes closed
stripped of human cloth, it is then, you cannot see celestial light.

Backward into past realities incite lost souls to continue lifeless flights
in desperate attempts to spiritually ignite nothingness
hidden lost and lonely inner visions
no eternal love, no soul mates, forever seeking false redemption.

Kindred souls woven together, life after endless life, seeking only pain
no virtue, no claims, inconsistent patterns of short-lived fame
darkened images in denial of life-giving solar light
mutant species spread across a boundless timeless universe of self-doubt.

Countless genetic numbers, cautiously awaiting a cosmic call to return
predictable rebirth cycles on display for your eyes only
needless to say, never mindful of truth
ingrained forever in abstinence, with so many lessons yet to be learned.

After ten-thousand years, most barely notice
life as a burial ground for fools
treacherous obstacle courses of self-deception
built on crumbling foundations of faith
not as to the true nature of GOD, but as an out-of-focus self-image.

Solar light, our eternal radiation fading away,
as humanity will do, without a fight.

Skeptical ones, hear me out, there are spiritual stains in fortune and fame
outrageous stains to cleanse in rotating biographies of life
no exceptions, creatures reclaim life in rebirth
cycles, born of its name, karma.

Kid 4 Real

There are two-hundred and fifty million anguished voices
singing patriotic songs
disoriented
by
dancing to the beat of different drummers.

The tranquil and tormented, stepping side-by-side
crazed, dazed, hazed
glazed over
In
red, white, and blue wash 'n' wear.

Troubled by a welfare state, engrossed in criminal intent
with
a scent of money in the air.

Totem 'n' taboo, limited knowledge, prescription drugs
principled thugs
on alert
knowing diversion is the key to success.

Sugar coated gingerbread houses and aromas from the oven
everyone lovin'
the taste of American Pie
with the hard pits you are told to swallow.

A dehumanization of Our Town, born on the Fourth of July
a virtual reality
like
Lucy in the sky with diamonds.

There are no realities, everything is an illusion, all is vanity
for the sake of sanity
everything under the heavens has a time.

The sun shines bright in my corner of the world … I am Kid 4 Real.

Large Walls, Small Houses, Little People

... It's a crying shame, no one sees a realistic
danger, in the American dream ...

Did you ever notice hippies from the 60's, with those gaudy mail boxes
it seems they live on the road less traveled
kinda makes you think
their out-of-date lifestyle, would be a serious threat to urban America.

Welfare recipients cash government checks the first of every month
sell cocaine to make payments on wire-wheeled Cadillacs
must be the high cost of transportation
to take fourteen kids with different names along for the ride.

Social security checks, endangered species like old revolutionaries
it's not cool man to spend those buffalo nickels
many years ago federal agencies
developed cataracts
when it came to seeing desperate needs of the disenfranchised..

Hey, more is less, less is poverty, trade in your overdrawn credit cards
the federal government loves to recycle charity
it's good for the economy
super rich elite get 90% kickback, even in depression era times.

Genuflect, count rosary beads and take a hallowed leap of faith
keep those offering plates full
Catholic sorcery can't make manmade saints
wine, crackers, holy refuge, catacomb finder fees, an unknown lower world.

Mary, Mary, quite contrary, your garden has grown unsightly
noxious weed, Eucharist seeds, hundred dollar bills
adequately fertilized by decomposed religious artifacts called Christianity.

Psychology 101: 21ˢᵗ century obsessions in Sigmund Freud, Oedipus Rex
college institutions hexed by uncontrolled primal sex
must be the water, cannon fodder, or holy wars
husbands, wives, children, run for your lives,
religious killing fields breed spores!

Large walls, small houses, little people, as far as the eyes can see
angels on a half shell, baked or steamed, life
goes on, another outback erotic hell.

*~ Insatiable-Insatiable-Insatiable-Insatiable-
Insatiable-Insatiable-Insatiable ~*

Isn't Life Strange

Keys turn in every lock
as
shock waves
puncture human brain cells.

How near yet so far we seem to be
from
the transcendental reality we seek.

The herald angels sing, as flapping wings
slap against our head
so, it must be said: we are more alive than dead.

Portals in ethereal time allow us this fragmented realism.

Mental landscapes of frozen waters
from
so many past lives
overflow the banks of our shallow emotional creeks.

So metaphysical and remote
such lasting hope
floating in endless frigid space, as we sprinkle stardust.

Behold, the man and his bride
spanning centuries
trust
peace and love
has only increased the flames of fragmented realism.

Centuries of waiting for just the right time
sends shock waves
soulmates gaze into future years
silently, keys turn in every lock, in mock concern I ask: Isn't life strange?

MARTIAN CHRONICLES

I saw a little guy with big eyes
stare out at me
from
the window of the local JC Penney store.

Eyes so large I was supercharged
eyes so bright
in
the middle of the night.

I stared at the face, I couldn't erase the image.

Without warning, before I could focus
on the scene
he disappeared
without a word, without a trace.

I clamoured after him, I stammered in despair
I looked everywhere
it was as if
he just vanished into thin air.

Sometimes, late at night
most often
at
the foot of my rumpled bed
somehow, they appear out of nowhere.

I am certain good news will arrive
for all of you
some day very soon
then you will be as amazed as I was, the first time.

Then as now
if you are free of mortal doubt
you will have no fears about, reading the Martian Chronicles.

Mary, Mary, Quite Contrary

What strange crop rotations after an investment
in "Better Homes and Gardens"

Tinker Belles, cockle shells, inflatable dolls, lost souls, the rapture
did you take the time
to correctly read instructions on earth harvest?

Drawn to simian calls, hitting heads against walls, they do it all again
no lessons learned
cry and pray, simplest way no rule of thumb
hands in the air, with middle finger extended, to chase away karma.

Tattooed, standing in a row, the show that never
ends, postcards from the edge.

Eastern, western, offering plate, emancipate, posterity, act of fate
watching everyone copulate, don't push, don't shove
no room at The Inn, where wise men gather
only selfsame names, etched in blood
once again, nailed against the wall, signed, sealed, delivered.

The final bell tolls, all church bells ring, all begin to sing holy songs
It is said: dirty deeds are done dirt cheap
no reality check, no sense, no reason
bound and gagged, earth, wind, fire, the world conspired against you.

Merrily, merrily, row your boat, sink, swim, simple choice, rejoice
living reckless, those who drown in hopeless schemes
hear the screams, shattered dreams
slippery rocks, electric shock, ignore all other tormented primal extremes.

Life is embedded in stone, as priests with beads, arouse sexual needs
so many changes in rarefied air, how many versions left to compare:
Adam, Eve, Amy, Steve
Adam, Steve, Amy, Eve
Oh, it makes me wonder, who is buying, who
is selling, the stairway to heaven.

Mary, Mary, quite contrary, welcome to the
sacred garden, how did it get so weird?

Me Knock 'n' Beggin'

Slowly moving, slowly thinking
Moving, thinking
In a lost and scattered, troubled past.

One by one
None alike, none the same
One by one, they frame our existence.

Two by two
None alike, all the same
Two by two, more or less, lost by name.

Broken up, one by one
None alike, all the same, all alone
Toward the closed door they all came.

One hundred and forty four thousand
Maybe more, maybe less
More or less, laughing, crying.

Maybe more, maybe less
Laughing, crying, living, dying
Laughing, crying, living, dying, more or less.

Tribe upon tribe, rich and poor
Rich and poor, nothing more
Gathering north, south, west and east.

Gathering as hosts of a biblical beast
North to south, west to east
Gathering by the thousands, maybe more.

In a lonely village, lost in time
In a place, no one can easily find
I am alone, me knock 'n' beggin' at the door.

Millionaires in Sneakers

Oh, say can you see biblical giants on TV? ...

Yes, indeed on TNT in the winter
Saint and sinner tune in
You don't get splinters in your rump!

Charles in charge and big Shaq attack
Larger than life and here's to your health
So much wealth it makes you want to puke!

Millionaires in sneakers above the rim
While parents skim by 9 to 5.

Please, give me a financial break
Nike and Reebok support millionaire jocks
You guys bake the cake and eat it too!

Kids brainwashed by NBA numbers and names
Laugh at parents and itemize fame
Pointing fingers of blame to satisfy needs!

Millionaires in sneakers above the rim
As dad and mom trim the budget.

A word to the lady who sits on many waters ...

Sons and daughters make parents suffer
There is no buffer in this game of greed
Moral seeds of corruption being planted deep!

When the bitter harvest is reaped
Red, white and blue won't get off cheap
An aborted American dream will be in la la land!

Millionaires in sneakers know
Commercials never show moral values in bare feet ...

Number Nine

Hey, the sound cabinets oughta be over there
I know Sonny and Cher
I definitely did this kinda gig before.

Don't push!! Don't shove!! Come on!! Start the show!!
I got these great seats in number nine row.

I'm gonna sing along with John ... I oughta be up there ...

I got candles, gonna pass 'em out to friends
Don't applaud
Just shake your jewelry.

Man, it's a heavy trip man, no one cares!
... Ya can't throw me out!

... I'm gonna get this program signed to show the world ...

Whatta ya say officer
A nothin' gig ... I feel like ... ya know ... a nowhere man.

John Lennon ... sure I know him ...
... Yah!! He lives at the Dakota 'round the corner ...

I got candles, gonna pass 'em out to friends
Don't applaud
Just shake your jewelry.

Ahhh, it's a personal joke officer ... a personal joke!

... Man, there's somethin' in the air
It's cold
In
New York City
I wish I did know Sonny and Cher ...

... Good evening' Mr. Lennon, could I have your autograph? ...

Patriotism Sets The Cost In Lives

Sway mightily, all you favored few, amongst the broken limbs
scattered about
the shifting sands of time
forever, to be seen no more, among the living.

Why worry, what is said in haste, it has no meaning to the fool
so very few
are touched by greatness
so many fall, into the ranks of the unknown.

Worry not, you are a mighty king, to whom the ignorant bow
here and now
fighting for their right to live
forever to be found, in corroded shackles of the rich.

Clearly, many things are lost that none can salvage, as their own
knowing bitterness lights many fires
within the heart
where only the destitute and huddled masses reside.

Dangerous are forbidden fruits, that fall around the tree of life
too much sorrow, too much strife
to overcome
fun loving souls, forever torn apart, in tragic wars.

All accommodate the whore, those experts of selected social breeding
drink you now a toast, to unsolved mysteries
carefree in knowing
those who too often listen, fall upon a rusted sword.

Bored with life, a mortal curse, that death brings to bear upon the living
non-forgiving souls, who cannot forget
who rebuke the truth
no compromise, only themselves to satisfy the need.

Another mighty king resides, astride a mighty steed, his message received
speaking in muted tones
no need too great, no hope too small
but all who listen, do not know, the price of freedom.

Patriotism, sets the cost in lives, inspired by
a profit, not words of the prophet.

Peace Unto You

Just stopped by your place to say hello
so mellow out
times they are a changin'.

Our 21ˢᵗ century world seems to be rearrangin'
the celestial room
isn't recognizable anymore.

I'm sorry I missed you, it's frustrating I agree
me knock 'n' beggin'
maybe you didn't know it was me.

I haven't changed much over the centuries
I've been told
churchyards added more crosses.

Please, don't count on me for your salvation
I'm a believer in God
how odd that you should doubt me.

I loved flowers and beads, we filled a need at Woodstock
I still talk about it
I guess God didn't fit into their plans.

So peace unto you man, until we meet again, somewhere in time.

Principle Of Peace

Man, it's space and time, psychedelic drugs, in a line
flower children
spouting out, loose fitting rhyme.

Someone sold the dream today
let's try
peace and love
another day, before I lose the feeling.

Time and space, hippies gone without a trace
too much
love and hate
whatever happened to reality.

All of you sold the dream, good-bye peace.

All of you have lost the feeling, good-bye love.

No one saw GOD behind the curtain, he wasn't there.

Come on people, pick the flowers, don't count the beads.

Hey you, don't spread these seeds of doubt, don't shout the name in vain.

Yes, I guess, liberty does ring true, for the chosen few
you know who you are
the lonely
the view from afar, from a far distant world

Pearls of wisdom, cast before swine, drink the wine
hide behind that curtain
you know
who you were, before the brainwashing began.

Pick the flowers, count the beads, the answer is in — the principle of peace.

Prophet On Wall Street

Open summer fire hydrants gushed water
The Big Apple
became an instant wading pool of freedom for the poor.

In downtown Manhattan brain dead fools
bathed in money
wagering the sum total of freedom in life, on profit and loss.

… Sages and soothsayers play the game, only
to live and die on Wall Street …

It was an incredible sight to see, suddenly inside The Stock Exchange
a long-haired bearded guy appeared in aisle three
wearing a robe and sandals.

Investors screamed and cried
"Who is this crazed, long-haired bearded guy?"

Tables flew in the air and frantic moneychangers fell over chairs
ticker tape machines scattered everywhere
in
full view of the rich and famous.

No one could explain how he got into the sacred pastoral room
moneylenders assumed
mind altering drugs gave him the power.

Just as quickly as he had appeared, he disappeared into thin air
shaky voices sighed
"he vaporized before our eyes."

Some claimed New York City was shrouded in a ghostly haze
some insist
the day was staged by the Actors Guild.

It was unfathomable to imagine
and
impossible to believe
the story was retold countless years, to anyone who would listen.

The Guilded Lady who stands upon many waters
laid down her torch
just long enough to pray, that on The Judgment
Day ... justice will wear it's blindfold.

Pursuit Of Happiness

So delicate and fragile
in
their own mind
like decorative iron in stained glass.

Passing among the people
laden
with untold riches
in a class all by themselves, marking time.

Words alone cannot describe
so many
yet so few
the wonder of wonders.

Fortune and fame claimed them as heroes
so very long ago
anyway
you know of whom I speak.

Nameless, mindless, status freaks
who tried to squeak
past
the timeless eternal door.

Sad to say, for those who strayed
the quest for truth
was
never very far away.

I must confess, pieces to the puzzle
are lodged
inside your own head.

In the pursuit of happiness, solutions to basic
moral issues, was never found.

Rumpelstiltskin

Once upon a midnight dreary
I heard
a thousand scary creatures wail and cry aloud.

Crowded corridors
filled with
shouting angry people waiting to see the sly dwarf.

What do they see looking at his strange haunted face
I know
a place in history has been set.

I have no regrets
for
feeling incapable to condemn him for what he did.

I cannot tell a lie, I realize
]the little elf
was
only practicing the art of self-deception.

No exceptions to the rule
only fools
allow weaker minds to misconstrue the mortal truth.

Mothers help tear down the wall
there is
a dwarf inside us all to incite mischief when we are small.

No self-effacing wall of fabricated charm
can save your soul
when
harm is done and life grows cold on the karmic path.

Stealing the child within
defines
one of the seven deadly sins wrought by morally corrupt men.

Rumpelstiltskin
lives in the minds of those evil men
the harbingers of hate who pretend to mend a broken child.

... Above all else, I curse this feeble-minded
elf, that mental midget in us all ...

Explain to me this game of fools
with kids in school
on the dead run dodging stray bullets to save themselves

Gnomes and elves invisible creatures lost
it's no coin toss
when it comes to classroom dominance and kids with guns

Tragic as it appears to me
no one
can pretend to be naïve enough not to see the danger signs

A total stranger to our hallowed shores
could not ignore
signals of the third kind being sent generation to generation

… The consternation of today does not play well with lessons shown …

It's difficult to believe Dr. Spock was proud
of
gathering clouds and hysterical crowds too many to imagine

W riting A rithmetic R eading
is
feeding on the groping minds in need of proper nourishment

The key to abate swirling winds of hate
is
the simple act of love
take the time to discipline your child without push and shove

Teachers need to learn
how
to make the kids yearn for common sense lost in frantic lives

Please, dear God, come back to school
don't let them be fooled
by
educated salvation that ends beneath the marble tree

... School days, school days, what ever happened
to the golden rule days? ...

Seven Deadly Sins

If there is a place for us in the universe
then why
do we feel all alone?

Is it the bone that was thrown into the air
you know
the one I keep talking about!

Is it all in the wrist or just a twist of fate
when man elevates himself
to
the status of God?

Is it an illusion or merely a delusion of grandeur
those things
that
spur us on to glory and fame?

Snug as a bug in a rug
waiting
for
the vacuum cleaner of life to inhale us.

How poised and ready
we are
to jump in front of the beater bar of fate.

Jaded as this may sound to you
we all knew
the day of reckoning would come much too soon.

We put a man on the moon and saw a face on Mars
unaware
emotional scars run deep.

... What are these Seven Deadly Sins, that humans view as truth ...

Rock 'n' roll legends praised Aquarian mystics
who gave tormented painful birth
to
unique new species
of
peace 'n' love.

Flower children encircled the globe
drawn
by
the timeless hope of a new spiritual redemption.

Music of the spheres echoed inside head 'n' heart
a
celestial start
silenced
by
the tragic loss of a dream.

New vibrations, suppressed sensations, hallucinations
altruistic sublimation
alienation
in
a love starved hippie generation.

Love beads, eastern religion, quest for cosmic power
all devoured
by
psychedelic drugs.

It is sad to recall after all the hopes 'n' dreams
the Woodstock nation
of
peace 'n' love
lived 'n' died in one motion.

Love was slowly replaced
by
the years of spiritual waste left behind on the Seven Hills of Bethel.

Ship of Dreams

Memories of things that never was
spread rapidly
like
warm ripples in a cold stream
splashing upon distant and unknown shores.

I listen with caution to the raging silence
of
the water
swirling deep below.

… I am comfortable numb inside …

All my dreams built on haunted castles
made of sand
all
washed away in the sea of hope.

When if ever I return to this place in time
hopes and dreams
would be
vague images of better days.

I think I cried as I prayed
knowing
no one warm ripple came back to me today.

~~~ It was as if my ship of dreams sank into the murky deep. ~~~

Shock the Monkey

OK, press the panic button
It's me again
And
Cretin is the subject for today.

Now class, sit quietly in your seats
While
I take the roll call.

All in all, I would say, today is a new beginning
We are winning
The war on ignorance.

Your willpower can be broken
I have spoken
About your shabby token efforts
Nothing to fear, but fear itself, just to thicken the plot.

A penny for your thoughts
If you have any
Well, I guess I've said enough about today's religion class.

If you philosophers survive the course
With
No remorse
I pray you find a way, to help your fellow man.

Do what you can, ban the bomb
Explain
How to stay calm, and love your neighbor.

Christians, in your lifetime
You will
come to understand the meaning of cretin.

The seating chart has been made
Don't be afraid
If you're a spiritual junkie
You can shock the monkey ... and board the mother ship on time.

Sigmund Freud

Think what we could do
if I was you
and
you were me
subconsciously, we would be as one.

Who can deny the past
nirvana
cannot last forever
walking on
karmic steps, unless we climb as one.

What would remain untold
protected
from the cold
together
if I was you and you were me.

It has always made me cry
to touch the sky
where
others have been
a new revelation, in time 'n' space.

To those who are lost again
mortal sin
has
no greater fury
than the lost years in our mind.

Distortions in a cosmic mirror
the looking glass
where
past and present
oddly resemble, craters on the moon.

The psychoanalysis of mutated alien genealogy by Sigmund Freud.

Some New Forgotten
Principles of Peace

Wow, man, like, another time and space, man, wow
traces of psychedelic drugs
you know the ones
all laid out
not in a straight white line
look around man, what has happened here
the flower children of Woodstock, have aged beyond their years.

Someone dark and ugly auctioned all the dreams away
someone fell to their knees and cried
bring back
peace and love today!
No way man, guns do the healing, smile before you lose the feeling ...

Time and space, hippies gone without a trace
not enough love, too much hate
what happened to reality?
Man, why did you hippies cease to dream, goodbye peace!

Maybe a forgotten feeling, someone lost the
feeling, or maybe it was never there?

Man, no one saw GOD behind the curtain today, HE wasn't there!
Come on people, pick flowers, don't count beads
hey you, don't spread seeds of doubt, whisper,
don't shout, it's a name, lost in vain.

Patriotism, the liberty bell only rings true, for a select few
yeah, you know who you are
The Lonely Ones
viewed from afar, from a far distant world, built on foolish dreams.

Pearls of wisdom, always cast before swine, they drink the wine

they hide behind that curtain.
Can you tell me who you were, who you were before the brainwashing?

OK, pick flowers, count beads, here are some
new forgotten principles of peace.

Somewhere Down This Hidden Road

An autumn breeze finds new bodies, swept along by the tides of time
so many lost lives, lost and nameless to most
yet so identifiable
by virtue of those, with whom they so solemnly dwell.

All those faceless smiles, forever lost in the backwash of a timeless hell
knowing full well they paid the price
free parental advice
relentlessly counting on those, who pushed them there.

Knowing inevitable unforeseen danger lurks, in raging hormonal fires
stirring glowing ambers of an unbridled desire
that was once smoldering flames
leaping high into endless nights, to satisfy human needs.

Out of mortal fear the names change, but the anger still remains
dangerous mindless rage, lurking deep inside
senseless vanity and pride
scratching, clawing, so hopeless, a never-ending quest.

Like an invisible armature, unbridled fear,
wraps around its intended victims.

Casting glances toward dark abandoned corners of the mind
framing all too familiar rooms
where nothing was ever said, that eased the pain.

Glistening across the shallow sea of time, in an uninterrupted space
asking why this silent disgrace, so humanly unbearable
to light new internal fires
forgotten rage, encapsulated in time tested directions of fate.

Emotional miles measure false steps in life, to
ease the pain that leads nowhere.

Castaway fabrics of lost memories, leave feelings of closure in seclusion
these elements of deception harbor no illusion
following lines of uninterrupted journeys
releasing pre-conceived endings on dreamers unaware of the dream.

Somewhere in a gathering circle of mist schemers seek repose
yet another chapter in the lost annals of life
the enemy isn't there, though in deep despair, the search goes on
somewhere down this well-hidden road, we find
detour signs in shattered schemes.

Teddy Bears and Lions

Around the room cameras zoom into focus
a dozen eyes
stare in wild desperation.

Two of them are mine
and
life is so sublime
listening to others define human isolation.

... Someone else in the room knows our secret ...

Pride and valor
in
relationship
to time and space as we know it.

Crazed senses outline human fear
parallel emotions
in
shadowed corners of our darkened room.

... Those childhood thrills in days of future passed ...

Protruding eyeballs separate tears from fur
preservation of hidden sanity
in
times long forgotten.

Our quiet chamber of sleep
transformed
by
voices silent and mute upon awakening.

We cannot refute unscrambled words of our friends

that return

from the outer edges of time.

... That lost wisdom of teddy bears and lions, we once again seek ...

Temples of Our Mind

I reach through dimensional windows into time
inclined to believe
insanity
has
finally taken man.

I am adrift in a lonely world of insane proportion
directions I have been given of late
appear
vague and unclear.

... A simple question: "Why have you forsaken me?" ...

I have no fear of this mutant world
it has
no spiritual appeal
it feels so unreal and lost in its own confusion.

Illusions plague those who walk with eyes closed
believers
pray in silence to be heard.

... Non-believers fall prey to the deafening sounds of nothing ...

No dictum by which man survives sifts through the lies
spiritual elements on any chosen path
leading to God
will be
strewn with unseen miracles.

Hear me now and allow these words to echo clear
God asks only what is fair
to anger slow
and
show others love and forgiveness.

This grants us a willingness to spiritually cleanse the temples of our mind.

The Circus Came To Town

New York City, the big apple, Madison Square Garden overflows
the 21st century Knickerbockers are on the road
this time traveling alone, nothing like it
drowning in the sorrow of pressure politics and professional sports.

Ahh, those smells of cheap perfume still numb the senses
a thousand small mindless faces
eagerly line up against makeshift yellow fences
staring at anything exciting, frightening, inside those worn out circus tents.

Tickets paid, bright lights, the greatest show on earth is beginning
large crowds beaming, countless number screaming
watching as human animal trainers hold back
the beast, with shaky broken chairs,

Oh my, check the sky, it's Batman, here to save
Gotham City, but you knew that.

What else on earth could compare, to the thrill of the crowd?
So, bang a gong, shake a tambourine, look skyward
don't forget to pray
make this terrible scene go away
people from everywhere, have come to see the circus.

Send in the clowns, listen to the noisy sounds of tortured joy
smiling as they playfully prance around
wherein laughter resounds
amid circling smoke clouds, against rafters, steel beams, or so it seemed.

So fast it was, uncounted miles, the long black train had traveled
it felt like it was only yesterday
but sad to say, it entertained you eager folks, making things go wrong today.

Ahh, the fascination of it all, was it a sin, that you crawled back in bed
feeling, knowing, you again relived an empty past
frown no more, no more worry
no sorrow, no grief, no life to relive, how very sad, that all seems.

OK, you knew this, those joyous events, like so many times before
all things must end, in either triumph or tragedy
so go ahead, wave flags, close doors
a cell phone to celebrate, don't stand by tall buildings, it blocks the signal.
When was it? Was it then, now or then, when
again the world turned upside down.

First a sumptuous feast, to feed the beast, that descending bird of prey
was it then, is it when, the fat lady sings, that the show is over?
The day the circus came to town, lame ducks,
fire trucks, just could not do enough.

The Godless Man

Demons in an ideological satire
Inflate the ego of unnatural desire
Crusted and uneducated brains bent and lame

Proclaim that evil is the way to solve the problem...

An even trade is God in an altered state
For children who rate themselves black or white
To study flight plans in the art of self-destruction

A production note from Egyptian temples of the dead...

Chemicals feather light and calorie free
Give a palatable respectability to the human brain
as materialistic gain lives and dies by cause and need

Shameless greed is the seed planted by the godless man...

The Good Earth

A vast expanse of land
Where people programmed to think
Stand on the brink of destruction
Lethal weapons drawn.

A world spins out of control
As loaded dice roll the final numbers
Those who slumber in unholy times
Exercise brawn over brain.

Knowledge shrinks each day
Moral values decay to pollute the good earth.

Wisdom between God and man
Is in the hands of those who plant the seeds.

Beat swords into plowshares and harvest the love …

The Human Zoo

Primal screams escape high walls around the zoo
Bouncing like rocks against empty caves
Exploding into future cosmic dust
Dark clouds of dust yet unseen by human eyes.

Human forms make animal motions through fear
Groping desperately at lost time
Becoming more like the animals
As each circle crosses another in spatial lust.

Golden hours ahead as busy hands fumble
To replace the mechanical digits
Set in constant motion by ancient clocks
Primitive rituals of lost time and molecules.

Secrets kept deep within the heart
Tumble out through the nostrils of faceless time
Fire breathing dragons fighting a final battle.

Gremlins of lost faith reside in the zone of mass confusion
Surrounded by barbed wire and stakes
That protect the holy relics of the past.

It is more blessed to give than to receive
Primal screams are everywhere today
Floating about us in invisible angelic forms.

Dust that circles fresh clean cages in the human zoo ...

The Idiot Box

Good morning kids
Those swollen eyes demand your attention
Now get away from the idiot box.

Nothing new under the sun
Shove, hit and run until the school day is out
Then take a direct rout to the idiot box.

There is no dispute about the fruit of its labour.

Kids are told what a bad day is
Stale corn chips and Pepsi that doesn't fizz
Their total knowledge from the idiot box.

Moral dispute of forbidden fruit on the idiot box.

Values come from mom and dad
That launching pad of future couch potatoes
Families live and die by the idiot box.

Happy Days and Leave It To Beaver
Discomfort for true believers in sex and violence
It makes the American Dream a living nightmare.

A bloody cross over the idiot box locks out the past …

The Judas Tree

Outlines against the sky
That never seem to fade away
Nor can it be denied by lack of hate

A revelation reaches deep inside the soul.

No control beyond tomorrow
Yet the images of yesterday linger
As in fleeting glances at the open cave

No more is mortal life compelled to grieve.

Brittle limbs across the sky
To stretch, bend and finally break
Shaken by the vital signs to subdue chaos

Havoc ruled the earth beneath marching feet.

Caution rules in seats of justice
Linked to those vital signs by visions
Decisions mock the fibre of the mortal soul

Though to all things there is a season
All things under the sun in view of the Judas tree...

The Traveling Salvation Show

Crumpled tents line our ancient travel routes
beside still waters
flowing from
the majestic Hallelujah River.

Weary eyes gaze now upon dry river beds
where holy waters
once ran
a swift but shallow course.

Dying branches sprayed in all directions
from
the Judas tree
jutting upward into the sky.

A sea of self-made gods in quiet repose
covered only
by
decaying foliage of the past.

Ten thousand years in hand hewn caves
slaves to emotions
and
causes of devotion unknown.

... Hinges of fate on doors of mortal fear rusted shut ...

Heavenly roads have been permanently closed
one reason throngs of angry protesters
headed for
The Talking Mountain.

The river runs through the fabled garden
The Tree Of Life
nourishes crystal clear waters
the traveling salvation show passes in review on its way to distant stars.

The Wake

No one knew his real name
Millions had a lame disbelief toward his earthly existence
The key to life is in our spiritual hands.

Curiosity seekers stared wild-eyed
Delirious viewers cheered at images on the evening news
He was admired, now no one seemed to care.

… Morning headlines read "he is dead and buried" …

A new rage in man by any other name
Designed to fit religious fortune 'n' fame, yet to die alone
Charades of faith edited for prime time ratings.

Closed coffin, no one viewed the body
Bawdy infidels set flags around the grave, no one cried
Signs implied desperate minds rejected peace.

… Parental guidance said "he is dead and buried"…

A hundred words or less were uttered
Someone muttered "he was not the same as you and me"
The tortured souls he set free, never shed a tear.

Smiles adorned the face of every mourner
The black vehicles approached the corner to the final exit
Perplexed voices seemed to fade, one-by-one.

… The words on the tomb read "he is dead and buried" …

Chronicles of a life besieged by mortal law
Remain a mysterious legacy to the cause of love unknown
Rolling Stone published rave review of the wake.

… A world away, miles from nowhere, he quietly celebrates his demise …

The World Inside

Desperate people pass by my door
Then
Run and hide
Without a sense of pride
Only a self-serving conviction to a mindless cause.

Water, water everywhere
And
Not a drop to drink
All those lost people teetering on the brink of reality.

Mortal eyes so blind they cannot see
They cannot find
The simplest truth in life
The one thing that gives them freedom from insanity.

... Isn't it rather frightening to you from the outside looking in? ...

Mortal sins you have committed
It's been said
Has made you grow old
Now you despise a life you feel you must defend.

What is the final cost, m memory loss, depression
Trembling at confession
While
The man in black makes nervous jokes?

You believe madness has driven you inward
There's no escape
No one can save you now
Maybe it['s better to say nothing at all.

It's come to the point
Where bitterness has overtaken your mind
You can't laugh, you can't cry, fear holds you prisoner to the world inside.

There Is No Reality,
Everything Is An Illusion

America, let us look at reality, it's the New World Order.
In God We Trust:
All others cash or credit cards
six billion lost souls cannot find any form of reality.

This is a reality: Do not pass GO, do not collect $200, or it's jail time.

We the people: Now there's a contradiction in reality
we the poor, give to the rich
making
rich people richer, while enslaving reality
a well executed plan in government deceit, corruption, and lies.

The government of the people, by the people, and for the people
shall not perish from the earth.
GOD knows:
Mr. Lincoln tried to make America face reality.

SO SEW SOW
Reap what you so desire the most:
"A house divided against itself, cannot stand."

George W. Bush created a reality Jefferson Davis only dreamed about.

Another reality of the times - Bye, bye, Ms. American Pie:
"And while the king was looking down
the jester stole his thorny crown
the courtroom was adjourned
the verdict was returned."

THE BIBLE, a book of forgotten realities
reincarnated
as manmade deceptions
those who know how the story ends, are the true authors of reality.

In reality: April 15 ... More biblical to America,
than all tax dollars collected.

To Further the Cause of Justice

Once upon a fearful midnight dreary
shadowy figures
told anyone who cared to listen
the greatest story ever told, about a ghost who walks.

Surely, you have all read this holy book
so many details for sale
minimum words
selling at maximum bargain prices
yet the loss of common cents, seems so little to ask.

Cast your lot among weary, wicked, hostile masses
sleep, maybe once more to dream
inside nocturnal thickets
where vaporized creatures, sing and dance, inside your head.

The work of true spiritual genius, to say the least
watching enraptured masses
feast upon the beast
morsels in the bread of life, to satisfy personal needs.

How do melancholy tales relate, to an unknown ghost
safely hidden in portentous clouds
governed as time eternal
thousands of invincible heavenly hosts, protect Top Secret files.

Oh, did I bother to mention, they don't drink
human blood from a holy grail?

I guess if all else fails, by Supreme Court decisions and human effort
believers could easily redeem lost faith
starting Latter Day Saint crusades, to raise
sufficient funds, for improbable wars.

No one knows, no spiritual growth, does anyone really care?
So, there it goes
heavenly hosts, lead us not into temptation,
until the new dawn of tomorrow.

Words are too often religious literary plums, to
bitterly further the cause of justice.

To Whom It May Concern

I guess it only seems fair
that
I should warn you
life will take on a new twist this century.

Anything and everything
will be seen
through the two-way cosmic mirror of life.

Roll the dice, take a chance and advance
around the board
but
don't pass "go"
don't try to collect $200.

You have heard me say many times
in
many ways
life is stranger than fiction.

I don't have addictions
nor do I find
an aversion to the truth as such.

Sonce we have learned
that
life reeks of lies
one must pray louder to keep the faith.

Though it seems trite
one might
be driven to a belief in the right of kings.

The theme of "Lord of the Rings"
I am sure
strikes a familiar bell
packaged to sell...postdated and labeled...to whom it may concern.

Uncle Sam

Uncle Sam calls it a mistake
A hundred bodies raked into unmarked open graves
Latest reports claim certain victory now.

Too often America turns it's head
Until the wounded and the dead are forgotten
There is something rotten in the way we misbehave.

Uncle Sam
Uncle Sam
That bearded old man in his patriotic zeal
Sets the seal of our republic upon shaky ground.

So rare the elements of truth
In those sacred temples and hallowed halls
Where Lady Liberty calls huddled masses to bear arms.

Greed and political wealth on the shelf
Guards a stealth flowing through amber waves of grain
Uncle Sam knows corruption stains a tattered flag.

Good morning, Uncle Sam!
What unholy stand does our Constitution take today?

Random acts of violence
Senseless displays of bitter hate
Totally separate us from the Universal Mind.

Uncle Sam
Count your beads behind those scarlet curtains
Tell us for certain heaven can wait.

Our American Cousin hides in dark prophetic shadows.

Wherever Did It Go?

Neighbors find no time to smile
for
even a short while
smiles don't seem to matter as the sun declines.

Biblical signs move slowly by the window
how simple
life appears to be today.

... On our way to nowhere, somewhere, everywhere ...

How fresh the spring breeze
spinning
those windmills we used to fight all night long.

Battles we may never win again
laughing
as though tomorrow is another sin to overcome.

... Knowing nothing, something, everything that counts ...

A thousand years from now
who
will remember
the craziness of our vows across the many hours.

Never have I ever seen such unhappy faces
life is good
could someone explain it to me?

I think, therefore I am
yet
the whammy
lurks around the corner despite our mortal cries.

Oh, beautiful spacious skies, it's mine forever, wherever did it go?

Printed in the United States
By Bookmasters